BOA
EDITIONS LTD

Ennui Prophet

Ennui Prophet

poems by
Christopher Kennedy

—⁓—

American Poets Continuum Series, No. 127

BOA Editions, Ltd. —⁓— Rochester, NY —⁓— 2011

First Edition
11 12 13 14   7 6 5 4 3 2 1

For information about permission to reuse any material from this book please contact The Permissions Company at www.permissionscompany.com or e-mail permdude@eclipse.net.

Publications by BOA Editions, Ltd.—a not-for-profit corporation under section 501 (c) (3) of the United States Internal Revenue Code—are made possible with funds from a variety of sources, including public funds from the New York State Council on the Arts, a state agency; the Literature Program of the National Endowment for the Arts; the County of Monroe, NY; the Lannan Foundation for support of the Lannan Translations Selection Series; the Sonia Raiziss Giop Charitable Foundation; the Mary S. Mulligan Charitable Trust; the Rochester Area Community Foundation; the Arts & Cultural Council for Greater Rochester; the Steeple-Jack Fund; the Ames-Amzalak Memorial Trust in memory of Henry Ames, Semon Amzalak and Dan Amzalak; and contributions from many individuals nationwide.

See Colophon on page 72 for special individual acknowledgments.

Cover Design: Sandy Knight
Cover Art: Robert Pollard
Interior Design and Composition: Richard Foerster
Manufacturing: McNaughton & Gunn
BOA Logo: Mirko

Library of Congress Cataloging-in-Publication Data

Kennedy, Christopher, 1955–
 Ennui prophet / by Christopher Kennedy. — 1st ed.
    p. cm.
 ISBN 978-1-934414-49-1
 1. September 11 Terrorist Attacks, 2001—Poetry. 2. Alzheimer's disease—Poetry. I. Title.
 PS3611.E557E56 2011
 811'.6—dc22
                      2010029673

NATIONAL
ENDOWMENT
FOR THE ARTS
A great nation
deserves great art.

BOA Editions, Ltd.
250 North Goodman Street, Suite 306
Rochester, NY 14607
www.boaeditions.org
A. Poulin, Jr., Founder (1938–1996)

State of the Arts
NYSCA

Contents

III

The trouble with our times is that the future is not what it used to be.
    —Paul Valéry

How smart are you?
How dumb am I?
Don't count any of my advice.
    —Paul Westerberg

I

No Wonder

As it happens, I was thinking how the earth curves always away, how we spend most of our time fighting gravity, how death leaves a body heavier, harder to carry, how we go through each day accepting this, how it's no wonder we pay to sit in the movie theatre so fear can jolt us and make our bodies lighter as our hearts race, as the hero conquers and the villain repents, and our eyes adjust to the absence of and sudden confluence of light, like a newborn's, and it's no wonder that we move differently in the dark, the false night unspooling around us, as the larger lives of others move to the music that closes down the evening, and we see only what we want to see.

—m—

The Fact Remains

I'm heavier than some animals, lighter than others. Also, I'm more threatening than most animals, less threatening than a few; faster than some, slower than most. I don't bite, though, unless provoked by desire. What I want to say is: I still measure distance in years. And swans mate for life. At least that's what I believe. I want a pair of *somethings* to refer to when I'm trying to make a point. The point is this: I'm an animal who knows where he stands among other animals. I can outrun a snail and threaten a housefly. I can conquer an anthill and mate for life. But the fact remains: My favorite dog has bitten the entire neighborhood. *Here, boy*, I say, but he ignores me, intent on running down another frightened child on a bicycle. He's mangy, too. His collar's too tight, and there's no quenching his thirst. Raw meat's the answer, but I'm too lazy to go to the store. This is the story of a boy and his dog. Though as far as I can tell, the dog ran off a long time ago.

—∞—

"Need Some Eyes for Your Next Puppet?"

Did you feel complicit when I began to shape the head of my next puppet? Did the way I covered the Styrofoam ball with cloth and tied it shut at the neck remind you how strange it is that we make something in our own likeness? Here are some eyes for my next puppet. There are several plastic buttons to choose from, or would you prefer I use the ones from my own head? And maybe I can cut off my lips and tongue and sew them to the puppet's face. And my ears and nose, they can be easily removed, and then attached to the blood-soaked cloth that is his head. If anyone comes to visit, I can put the puppet on my hand and let him speak for me. He can see what I no longer see. He can hear the questions I suppose are inevitable, the ones about why someone would do such a thing. Do you like the idea of a puppet that's so much like me? And more so the idea of me without my eyes, my lips and tongue, my nose and ears? I could sew some buttons over my sockets. I could paste on a macaroni smile. I could cut a piece of construction paper and shape a nose to tape on my face. I could do the same to make some ears. I could sit in total silence and show you what it means to be God.

—m—

Congruence

I hate to throw away fruit, so I stood in my yard with a bruised pear raised above my head, hoping to learn something about the human condition. A halo of bees, black- and yellow-striped, hovered, lazy in the late summer heat, in stasis, then orbited above the pear. Unable to pull free of the spoiled fruit's gravity, they swarmed and landed in a clump on a spot of deep brown, nearing black, drawn to the slow decay. They drank, then flew back to their nest, drunk with sweetness, slaked but not sated. There was still time for me to learn the importance of desire. I went back to the house and entered my data in a blue notebook, then spread myself with honey, hopeful and sticky beyond my ken.

—m—

Ennui Prophet

When I'm dead, I'll be eating mold spores, pine cones, sheaves of discarded paper. Or so I predict. I'm hours away from the door, years away from my next trip to the grocery store. The sun rises in the east like a Sumerian charioteer with bad news about the fate of Western Civilization.

I look out the window and think, *My eyes of half a century grow weary of the dawn* and immediately I feel ashamed. Gulls scavenge the rooftop puddles, miles from a reasonable body of water. Their cries the sound of a soul's rusty hinges.

If I think of it as meditation, my bedsores seem noble. I'm saintlike, therefore the long hair and beard. So what if I'm the king of the giant hamsters? Won't someone fashion me a proportionate wheel? And by the way, that's not a scream forming on my mouth; it's a yawn, though even I have trouble determining the difference.

The sun keeps insisting like a speed-freak panhandler who tells me his car has run out of gas. Yes, the merciless sun approaches. I'm immobilized by the daily bloodletting, the prayers that fall on deaf gods' ears. In any case, I know the future. It's predictable. It ends as it began, a complicated situation brought to light.

—∽—

Transubstantiation

In Pennsylvania, I unearthed a Mason jar, painted white, marked with the black shadows of blue herons. I looked inside and found a small skeleton, mouse or rat, some laboratory martyr, given a burial fit for a pharaoh. I smelled formaldehyde, a failed attempt at preservation. I took the jar home with me and set it on my bookshelf. I sat and stared at the shadows in flight until my eyes grew tired. I drifted off and dreamed I was falling, then flying, falling, then flying. I heard scratching from inside the jar. I opened my eyes. I waited to see what creature would emerge.

—m—

Grief Season

All summer there was a conspiracy to wonder. Blue was especially prominent. Then God sent the green wind, the sizzle and crackle of fallen power lines. The absence of light at night made the most sense. I really liked it when the moon waxed ominous.

In my sleep, I crawled through a narrow passageway, past the itinerant butchers and the saint of a thousand whores. I woke myself up from drowning and noticed the strange light of every day, crawling imperceptibly across the wall.

I sensed a wedding had taken place; a marriage had come and gone. I looked out the window at the smashed petals on the ground, where golden wasps, vaguely Egyptian, grew lazy, swarming the spoiled meat.

When I walked outside, I gathered a few fallen limbs and wanted someone to explain to me the meaning of eggshells and coffee grounds and attempted to feel okay about things. I heard a chainsaw in the distance, a truck shifted gears. I was almost back. Then a quiet sound caught my attention as if a blind carpenter were hammering roses.

—⁓—

Ghost in the Land of Skeletons

for Russell Edson

If not for flesh's pretty paint, we're just a bunch of skeletons, working hard to deny the fact of bones. Teeth remind me that we die. That's why I never smile, except when looking at a picture of a ghost, captured by a camera lens, in a book about the paranormal. When someone takes a picture of a spirit, it gives me hope. I admire the ones who refuse to go away. Lovers scorned and criminals burned. I love the dead little girl who plays in her yard, a spectral game of hide and seek. It's the fact they don't know they're dead that appeals to me most. Like a man once said to me, *Do you ever feel like you're a ghost? Sure*, I answered, *every day*. He laughed at that and disappeared. All I could think was he beat me to it.

—⁓—

My Mother Listens for Birds

Oddly, it's colder farther away, where the hottest things imaginable extinguish themselves. Outside my mother's window, the moon is a clock with no hands; the stars are bits of shattered glass from the windshield of my father's broken car. My mother's nerves unwind and rewind, braiding a static darkness in her veins; her purple hands flail as she asks the night what day it is. The night answers with sunrise; my mother listens for birds. She sees the post-dawn wash of rain that's stricken the fields. Behind the clouds, the sun burns only to burn itself out. A flock of memories scatters across the charcoal-colored sky. My mother watches the night settle in again, viscous and slick: the black mirror of a dead crow's eye. My mother listens for birds.

—〜—

Hypoglycemia

I knew a man who passed out with his hand in a jar of honey. I once convinced a stranger to give me his meal in a late-night diner. I said, *You're not going to eat that, are you?* He didn't say a word and handed me his plate. I ate his bacon and eggs as if they were my own. That's how hungry I've been. Last night, I ate in a chain restaurant decorated with black-and-white photographs of local buildings long torn down. More and more I trust strangers to prepare my meals. I'd waited too long to eat, so my blood sugar was a little low. The lamplight haloed the other customers as if they were all saints, and for a moment I felt like one of them until sweat began to bead on my forehead. I decided to order the daily special when the double doors to the kitchen flew open. A waitress attacked a family at the table next to me with a cake she'd set on fire. It seemed we were all supposed to sing.

—◊◊◊—

In the White Hour

for S.

White dust annihilates the windows: detritus of oaks, epidermis of kings. I'm riding the frayed gold couch toward a new world oblivion: king of whispers and bad luck. When the smoke clears, I'll buy you a reason to live if you promise to share. I'll rewind the tape so we can see every wrong turn in slow motion; freeze-frame your face and un-forget; gather the dust and recreate you; alter your perception of depth; save you from yourself; step out with you over the Grand Canyon.

Amish Radio

Wind travels around the world to speak its piece. A hurricane reaches shore. The sea untangles itself. A woman loses her mind. Willows slap their Buddhist limbs against the house. We hold our ears to the ground to listen for horses. There are four.

—⟋⟍—

Dream Horse

All day I wondered about the faceless horse from my dream, her wild dash across frozen ground as she stepped from her bridle, ears covered with a black sash. The presence of steam struck me most, steam above where her nostrils should have been, and the sense I had of a smaller horse, galloping in her womb.

—m—

II

End of the Ten-Foot Summer

Summer had been ten feet tall. It seemed endless, convincing us of our immortality. We came to terms with the inevitable when the blue sky grayed, turned pearly, opaque. Word spread. We decided to embrace the change. A few of us chose to be trees. Others imitated the sky. Hundreds gathered to simulate a field of wilted sunflowers, their heads bent toward the fallow ground. When the air cooled at night, we wondered when the frost would come. A few of us discussed the possibility of rebirth. That made us remember our children, who we hoped would go on without us. We knew they would. We knew we were taking the end of summer too seriously. We heard them laughing inside their houses, going on as if the change of seasons were the most natural thing.

—◊—

Church of the Holy Abattoir

I asked a dead cow her opinion of the slaughterhouse. She said she was confused at first; then she found peace. She was flayed and quartered by then, but when the dead speak, I tend to listen.

—w—

Act V

The trees of Dunbar began their march and never stopped. The prophecy keeps arriving, in perfect columns, outside your window, waiting for you to open the door. And you, you're afraid to move. You've never felt this way before: an axe handle seeking its blade, stiff and biblical with fear.

—∞—

"Wicked Go the Doors"

Moon-killers, a salt fuse lit by lightning, sulfur smell in the devil's lair; we'd go to the roadhouse, watch the rattlesnake eat its rock-and-roll tail; we'd speak in tongues and slither until the whole sick mess was as one in the eyes of no god; we'd speed until we were Jesus, hang by a cross made of thread; knew it was blindness wicked made.

—ᴍ—

The Year I Was Sick

Each day, I crouched in the corner where the last light comforted the red table. There was a sick animal that didn't know how to escape. It died inside me. I woke up several times a day from a different grave. There were internal filaments flickering, the sensation of a good story being told around a campfire in the concept of the Old West. I talked to a stranger who was me. There was a phone that kept pretending it was asleep. I knew better than to pick up the receiver. There was always another voice, another questioning substance. I believed in the curative powers of steam. Most of the things I did were things you do with your mind rather than things you do with your hands. Anything else that was done was done to me. While I sat in the dark, I learned to disappear, floating words aimlessly away from my mouth that was no longer two lips surrounding a darkness, but the darkness itself. I know this because no one heard me, and as I look back on the year I was sick, that's the reason I was cured.

—m—

Questions of Metaphysics

A one-armed man carries a hammer through the downtown streets. His empty sleeve pinned to his side, like a vestigial wing, he crowds the regulars who wait at the Centro hub for the 5:15. To him, their faces are wilted flowers in the deep sleep of his waking dream. He saunters back and forth, as if in search of a bell or the pedestrian nail. He stops, stilled by movements in the crowd, his synapses slowed by something blue. Each nerve knit to one filament of want within him, humming before the hushed crowd, he explains his senseless hammer.

—m—

After Christmas

I wore my snakeskin socks and a renewed sense of shame. I would have prayed, but somehow it seemed sacrilegious among the perfect arrows of pine, displayed in rows on the scattered swells of paper we'd torn apart so greedily. I embraced the spirit and built my model airport on the floor. With great precision, I placed the hangar in the northern quadrant of the room and lined the planes on the runway grid, careful to set a mechanic next to the landing gear of each. After the scene was complete, I stood the passengers in line at the terminal and scrambled for the sofa's higher ground, where I drew a bead with my Winchester replica on the tiny woman, pushing a yellow baby carriage.

—∭—

"Are You Looking for the Self-Help Section?"

We're hurtling along, incomprehensibly, on this rock, and there are many of us, including remarkably small versions of our larger selves. Today some of us are strewn among rows of shelves in uncomfortable silence, ashamed of our coffee and tea's inadequacy, embarrassed by the employees' enthusiasms, and we are forced, each of us, to look up from the book we pretend to read to watch the slow drift, the bright erasure, and walk around in it, as if in seeing with a dead eye from a dead self we can be brought to a higher place, exalted, the luminous aura of the flame's shadow we dream is inside us somehow burning a hole through our husks of flesh, through which we must pass to pass through ourselves, impossibly, if we are to do more than simply burn.

—⁓—

Museum of Wrong Turns

Here's something for everyone: cowboy boots worn by former presidents. See the various shoe sizes through the centuries. Don't let diminutives deter you from admiration. In the boxing hall of fame, the largest fists don't always belong to the greatest champions.

And here's to the roommate who thought Mt. Rushmore was a natural phenomenon. *What a coincidence*, she said, proud of her powers of deduction. And I defend her right to be so wrong. The colors of America are bright, its music spins me out of control, and the school system's a mess. What chance did she have, really? I envy her her sense of wonder.

To prove I can get with the program, I've purchased an expensive vehicle, fur-lined, all-wheel drive, to take me to the top of any mountain. I'm headed west this weekend to ruin as much of the pristine forest as possible. In no time, I'll be perched atop Lincoln's head, popping wheelies on his scalp, where I'll fire round after round from the semi-automatic rifle I pried from the *cold, dead hands* of a fallen icon.

—m—

The Brown Heroin of Love

A bouquet of wild dogs behind my back, I'm here to celebrate a rise in my cortisol, a decrease in my serotonin. There are ecstasies and then there are ecstasies. This isn't one of them. This is the brown heroin of love, the pure injection of irrational thought. I set a thousand redwoods on fire to demonstrate the neural circuits that control my social judgments are completely suppressed. I made a necklace out of live crabs because I know how much you love the sea. I may be looking in the mirror when I speak to you, but that's a quirk you'll soon find endearing. Look, the dogs are hungry, my dear. I can feel them gnawing through me to get to you. Accept what I have to offer, my lovely mirage, so these hungry dogs can have their way.

—ɷ—

The Day Before My Violin Broke

The wings of crows were quills dipped in India ink. I looked up from my lesson and watched them rise and bank in the wind, as they painted the pale sky black.

—ɯ—

Aloha

I stared directly at the sun for the prescribed amount of time. Sunblind, I stumbled inside to self-destruct. A constellation of lights sent me God thoughts. I deferred. I held out my hands to feel for the sharp edges of furniture. To be honest, I could see the whole time, but mine is a life based on exaggeration. I picked up the phone and dialed the number I'd memorized from a Honolulu Men's room in 1966. I told myself six rings; I told myself it doesn't matter if the number's wrong, that the truth is sometimes written in the dark. There was a voice at the other end that sounded like sunspots. I cleared my throat and prepared for the rest of my life. I fell to my knees and forgot how to pray. Hello, I said, which also means good-bye.

—ɯ—

The Rise and Fall of the Middle Class

Despite the beggars' shopworn vernacular, the perennial fits of anxiety, and the paranormally bright orange sun, I'm eating on the sidewalk with some aplomb. Speaking of screen doors and submarines and paving the road to hell. What does a full stomach have to do with any of this? Only that I make the case that good digestion could be an influence. The omelet Parisienne, burning now as fuel, feeds the brain and *Voila!* which is French for *In your face!* The red buildings are draped with strings of electric lights. This most festive July ever hangs, like a black cloud over the city. All this to say, *I'm a little depressed; pass the ammunition.* All vagaries aside, the moon will make a splendid plate to set the table of the sky. Maybe then the hungry mouths can feed. How is it I never remember the weatherman's lesson? What is it again he says at night just before I drift off to sleep? Oh, yes, of course: It's not the heat, it's the humanity.

—m—

Song of the Elysian Troubadour

It's the silence you can't explain just before sleep. Think of everything that never happened, that heaviness. Imagine a small skull sits in your palm. Multiply it by war. I dare you not to think of children fallen in the sand. That heaviness. Hold it in your hand, the skull. Close your fingers around it. Now you have the fist you've always wanted.

Why

Jack called to say he and Pete would be there before it got too late. You stood at the window and said, *Come look at the moon.*

There were bullfrogs croaking about flies and humidity loosening the skin from the dead. I was hoping for the sounds of rescue or restraint, the twangy guitars of yesterday, tuned to a minor key.

You said maybe I should wait outside where my pacing wouldn't make you nervous. I never thought of it that way, but I opened the door just to be polite.

The moon was a blood crescent, hanging like a meat hook in the pale sky. A strange blue car was parked next to mine.

It seemed they were out there, same as our lost cat. We shook hands. Pete scooped up a toad and offered it to me. I politely refused it. We were smiling, like it was a funeral for a relative we didn't know very well. You never went to the door. I had the feeling that meant something, like a feint pain in a nervous limb. I stood there, thinking for a while, like a priest with serious doubts.

Jack just kept saying good-bye.

—w—

Salt City Solo

Crucible's furnace sears a nuclear sunset in your eyes. "Voices" in the player spark a jumpstart chainsaw. You're headlong past the dead lake's moonlight spasm, channeling the nearest alien star. Green beds made of chemicals have been limned for you. You're injected. You wake up inside your father's steel coffin. Your eyes adjust to the curtain of flames. No one can prepare you for the next release. The next release shall be solo. The next release shall contain no electric guitars.

—m—

III

Searching for Ancestors

Maybe they're part of a plot to return to the sea, having grown tired of walking on two legs. Maybe they've held their breath so long they've grown gills, their hands and feet webbed, their bodies edged with silver scales. Maybe they're gliding underwater in the dead lake my father passed each day on his way to work. Maybe the water reminds them of their journey on the coffin ships. Maybe they look past the mirror of the lake's gray surface and imagine they can leap to the sky.

Wherever they are I hear them before I fall asleep at night, keening their grief, and I dream of them, bobbing to the surface, eyes and mouths wide open, like sick moon-fish under the stars, singing to me to swim.

—m—

Down to the Sea in Sinking Ships

I wasn't surprised to see the ships sail off the edge or to hear the predictable screams of the passengers. They had been warned repeatedly not to discover a newer world than this one and were served right. Theirs was the worst kind of shame: a reliance on scientific methods when circumstances demanded faith. I whispered a prayer to them as I offered my hand. When that didn't go over, I placed my finger on my wrist and held my arms above my head, reminding everyone of the aerobic advantages of an elevated pulse. They ignored me and continued to flail against the rising waves. *Watch me swim*, I yelled, like a child to his mother. It's true, I was near the shore, my feet were on the ground, and I was only pretending, but I remain convinced the message was still the same.

—m—

Stopped by Cops in South Carolina Where
the Billboards Shift from Jesus to Porn
and Back Again, I Understand My Affliction

It's as American as the F.B.I. Hoover in drag, a zealot in silk stockings, careful not to smudge his lipstick as he reads me my rights. The desire to reach the heavens gets mixed up with the pursuit of naked flesh, and the next thing I know, I'm ordering coffee and apple pie à la mode in a topless diner, next to a Bible salesman who can't get enough of those free refills. Halleluiah! Can I get a waitress? One who was at the scene of the crime? That's the easy part. It's as simple as a right hand and a left. I'm guilty of human needs. And here the billboards remind me, like flashcards for a five-year-old, alternating Lust and Love. Moving too fast is what got me here, stopped on the side of the road. The cops wear mirrored shades to keep their own sins hidden. The sign I'm next to features Jesus ascending and a 1-800 number to call if I feel alone. But I'm more hungry than lonely, and once I get my ticket, I'm gone.

—m—

They Are World Travelers

I'm sick of them arriving on the backs of rogue elephants, and I tire of their stories of aborigines. I burrow in my basement while they traverse oceans. When I visit them, I sit in chairs made of rare bamboo and mispronounce, while they speak fluent Cantonese, a rare dialect, spoken only by a cohort of twenty on a remote, exotic plateau that can only be reached on foot.

Dishwashers are a type of marsupial, I've decided. So I carry several photographs of my own to show at their dinner parties. They feign interest and project their slides of an ancient fertility ritual, involving the pregnant bellies of black widow spiders they say improved their sex lives yet again.

Their papaya sorbet tastes like dung, but I'm forced to smile and watch them hula across the living room in authentic Hawaiian garb. If only their skin were a different shade of umber; if only I weren't reduced to tears by the stories told by their bodies' sway and the graceful movement of their pertinacious, birdlike hands.

—⁂—

Post-Romantic Post-Mortem

The clouds last evening: white, bountiful, against a field of cerulean sky. A boil of hawks darted above me. A doe nursed its fawn in the bowl of grass next to the on-ramp. Telephone lines stretched beyond the clouds, a sign of our species' progress.

This morning, the fawn sleeps alone in the shade next to my house. Waves of guilt pass through me like a swarm of hypodermic needles, like a wedge of black swans, or a shower of razor-tipped arrows. The fawn will last the day, maybe the night. Tomorrow, I'll find it on the side of the road, rent by crows.

But right now, the moon bleeds orange, visible at the horizon, to prove that beauty issues from the coldest, most distant places, briefly and without regard for shame.

—◠◠—

Still Some Interest in the Heathen Gods

If only for the variety, the possibility of thunder and sunlight, the harsh winds, all having other names and purpose to their senseless chores. The sea come crashing could have a face and hold a trident, and I could know my body speaks of creation and destruction, understand my hands to be two iron hammers when closed tight and two mad flowers when they bloom out of love for another god-stricken soul.

—◊—

Humor Is the Arbiter of Sadness

A clown points a gun to his head; a chameleon stares at a plaid shirt. Some hired hands sail to India to prove the world is round and still we all fall off. A cunning use of light and shadow turns day into night and back again. There's nothing to do and a thousand ways to do it. I remove my well-worn shoes and send them into exile, two little orphans made of cow my bare feet had grown to love.

—⁂—

Rasputin's Folly

At night, when it's snowing, horses clomp down an alleyway, pulling a carriage crammed with exiled dignitaries. I walk to the window to see if God is dead. If he is, he's turning in his grave, which raises the question: *Can God dig a grave big enough for him to fit?*

I try to remember The Alamo, but I'm afraid of history. Those who are about to die need more than my salute. Mad Monk, were you sent by God to heal Aleksandra's son? More likely you were a source of unreliable information, yet somehow I still find your beard intriguing. But it did end badly, didn't it? The peasants, all jacked up on philosophy, ready to trade one form of oppression for another. And those novels, some of them over a thousand pages! I'm tired just thinking about war. Who has time for peace?

That doesn't mean I've given up on America. I'm a sucker for red, white, and blue. And I've got stars in my eyes, an eagle in my heart. You were considered a wolf in sheep's clothing. What can you tell me about the wolves dressed as wolves? Undress them and nothing changes. And is there some way to explain to the lambs that innocent blood won't sanctify? Rasputin, my friend, I'd hide them away, but they're all in line for the slaughter.

—m—

My Argument with the World, Part 3

At dawn, birds make inadequate attempts at song. I open my window and offer a critique. A starling dives at my head. No one likes to hear the truth shouted from a window at six in the morning, but I go about my business, knowing I'm correct, unafraid to face the day. By noon all my windows are dark with birds. I reconsider my opinion. *Birds*, I say, *if you can hear me, I've begun to understand the nature of your song.* Gradually, light begins to crawl across the floor in small, sparrow-shaped patches. I've betrayed myself, but who really cares what birds think? I walk over to the neighbors to complain once again about the music playing in my head. Some cranes fly over, silent, weighing their many options.

—m—

Where Does the Carpathian Highway Roam?

Heidegger wore a bathing suit, or so I assume. All the great thinkers sunbathed when no one was looking. Who doesn't have a little island in the tropics somewhere in the vicinity of their northern township? I'm thinking of England now, rainy skies over quaint wooden bridges. Which doesn't answer the question: Where does the Carpathian Highway roam? Not through this noisy historical moment but somewhere in the Urals perhaps. I'm only guessing based on my perceptions of the nether regions on my fifth-grade map. Aren't we all victims of the limited perspectives of the lowest rung employees at Rand McNally? That shade of pink China was forced to wear reminded me of an upset stomach and its popular cure. Here I go again, opening my friends' medicine cabinets under the pretext of concern for their well-being. Let's face it. I'm up for a good scandal even at the expense of the ones I purport to love. And if that makes me an American, so be it, so be the apple pie of pornography and unfit mothers. All the great thinkers had mothers who walked the floors with them, soothing their precious brain matter with camphor and lullabies. And so the highway roams in spite of my ignorance, and somewhere a baby begins to form a theory that puts two and two together. The maps evolve and the world gets a makeover. All the great thinkers walk the floor with their idiot sons and daughters. No one knows where the Carpathian Highway roams.

For My Students

One thing about having made mistakes, having, in fact, a long track record of having made mistakes, is that when one makes another mistake, it is almost a relief, almost a lifting of a heavy burden of correctness that one must bear until, unbearably, one must walk out into the street and confront a moving vehicle despite knowing (softly, like snow falling on more snow) the odds against winning.

—⁓—

Tombstone Hand

Tombstone hand and a graveyard mind
—Ellis McDaniels

The left-handed guitarists were always in danger. The left-handed guitarists died on the midnight crossroads, their words bruised into women's names and unforgivable desires. The hand held over them was black and voodoo and full of calcified love. Their timeworn riffs fade to the static between stations, as if that hand tuned a dial inside you, scanning the radio waves for a demon sound that breaks from the deltas and the swamps, like a fever that burns and aches your body all night long, all night long, and you wait for whatever is changing to reach a clear frequency, a new song that plays for a few minutes on the radio, the latest variation on the Diddley beat: *Who do you love? Who do you love?*

—m—

A Vague Memory of Wings

A swarm of bees followed me home last night. Winged, pollen-laden, branch-haired. Everywhere I walked, bees shadowed me. When I stopped for dinner, the swarm hovered outside, waiting for me to leave. It looked like a dark cloud, which made me think my luck might be turning away from me again, manifested in the ominous merger above my head. When I arrived at my house, the bees were undeterred by doors or walls and flew behind me into my bedroom. When I lay in bed, trying to sleep, the cloud circumambulated the room. The bees seemed to have an urgent message or a warning. I could sense they wanted something from me. What it was, I couldn't tell. I wondered if the swarm was really something else, maybe my father's soul or the soul of an old friend. Or maybe my mother's soul, though she's still living, stuck in a papery version of the world.

As I ruminated, the bees formed two lines and flew into my ears, where they crowded my head like thoughts of a long drought. My dreams were shadows of dreams. There were human figures, gesturing from far away. I saw them as if through a screen door in summer. They were telling me to follow them somewhere I was afraid to go, as if I were a child again, unsure of the world and my place in it.

I slept fitfully, waking up often and looking around the room for the source of the noise inside my head. I sensed a low humming sound but thought nothing of it. Something electric was doing its job. When I woke the next morning, I had a vague memory of wings, an image from one of my dreams still lodged in my head: the hive in flames, the queen asleep in her chamber.

—✲—

The Unimaginable World

If I stab you with the crescent moon, you can't be mad at me. You can be surprised, but not angry. No one can admonish me for using the moon as a weapon. In the unimaginable world, a moon stabbing is perfectly acceptable. I know this type of romance takes patience. I'm busy in so many realms, I'm not always available. I sleep with my eyes open so I can keep you amused.

If I smother you with a rain cloud, it's just another illusion. Don't hold it against me. None of it's real. I'm throwing stars at you, but you don't even feel it. I've crushed you three times today with a mountain, and you go on as if nothing happened. I rose from the dead just to see what's for dinner. I slipped though the silk membrane of time so you wouldn't have to sleep alone tonight. I'm body and blood. I'm the good with the bad. I'm not what you think when you think you're thinking about love.

—ɯ—

Rara Avis

My mother was born with wings on her ankles. She's been cutting them off since she could hold a butcher knife. They grow back. She cuts them off. She can't fly. The wings are useless. They reappear with the promise of flight, the false hope of escape. She tries to ignore them. They itch like scabs. She cuts them off. She dreads the day she loses her strength and lets them grow untamed. She fears she might be tricked by the arc of their shadows into believing in their power, the moon and the stars inviting her, the open window examining her faith.

—⁓—

Mandala

The Buddhist monk inside my head sifted colored sand into landscapes that blew away in a gust of wind. No matter how beautiful the ochre or how stunning the cobalt blue, no matter how hard I tried to hold the picture in place, the sand was here and gone.

I concentrated one final time to help the monk finish. I forced his hand to move the metal funnel to shape a palace and a lotus on a bed of jewels. When he finished, I took one final look before he rose and put away the funnel. I could barely see the mandala as he ran his knuckle through the scene. I clung to the image for a moment; then it was gone.

The monk burst into flames.

—ɷ—

Waking Up at the Wheel

I woke up behind the wheel and told my wife I'd been talking to Good King Wenceslas. A giant red ant wearing a crown figures in this story, as do the taillights of an eighteen-wheeler. The difference between living and dying and the mathematical certainty of one or the other happening to all who have been small, shivering things, also included. The median and the darkness of the southern tier, the rest areas seen and forgotten, the deer timidly nosing their way past the scrub pine toward the shoulder, the orange glow of the truck driver's cigarette in another poem in Arkansas, they are involved as well.

The conversation was simple. The King asked me why I was asleep, and I told him I wasn't. I told him I was seeing from behind my closed eyes and that he was a vision of great importance. That's when my wife asked me a different question that required my full attention, and I woke up, just in time to see two deer about to make a bad decision.

—⚶—

Acknowledgments

Grateful acknowledgment is made to the editors of the following print and online journals in which these poems first appeared, some in different versions:

The Associative Press: "Questions of Metaphysics";
Cavalier: "They Are World Travelers," "The Unimaginable World," "Mandala";
The Collagist: "'Are You Looking for the Self-Help Section?'";
Dogzplot: "In the White Hour," "'Wicked Go the Doors'";
Dossier: "My Mother Listens for Birds";
Hobart: "Museum of Wrong Turns";
In Posse Review: "Where Does the Carpathian Highway Roam?";
New York Tyrant: "Aloha," "Ennui Prophet," "After Christmas," "My Argument with the World, Part 3," "Ghost in the Land of Skeletons," "A Vague Memory of Wings," "Why," "Searching for Ancestors," "Congruence," "The Brown Heroin of Love";
Ninth Letter: "'Need Some Eyes for Your Next Puppet?,'" "The Fact Remains," "Waking Up at the Wheel";
Opium: "Down to the Sea in Sinking Ships," "Stopped by Cops in South Carolina Where the Billboards Shift from Jesus to Porn and Back Again, I Understand My Affliction," "End of the Ten-Foot Summer";
Pacific Review: "Tombstone Hand," "The Rise and Fall of the Middle Class," "Grief Season";
Redactions: "Rara Avis";
Stone Canoe: "Rasputin's Folly";
Willow Springs: "No Wonder".

I would like to give special thanks to my wife, Mi Ditmar, for her careful reading of this manuscript.

Thanks to my editor, Peter Conners, for all his good work.

My gratitude to Sarah Harwell for her insights and patience.

Love to Tessa and Louisa and to Margeaux, Chase, and Harrison.

As always, love to Steph for her friendship.

Thanks to David and Lija Ditmar for their kindnesses.

Thanks to Gian DiTrapano for his support.

Thanks to Steve Keeler and to the Cayuga Community College Foundation for their generosity.

And thanks to Robert Pollard, Rich Turiel, Sandra Knight, Richard Foerster, and Jay Muhlin.

The Paul Westerberg epigraph is from "I Will Dare," The Replacements, *Let It Be*, Restless Records (1991).

—◁▷—

About the Author

Christopher Kennedy is the author of three poetry collections, *Encouragement for a Man Falling to His Death* (BOA Editions, Ltd.), which received the Isabella Gardner Poetry Award in 2007, *Trouble with the Machine* (Low Fidelity Press), and *Nietzsche's Horse* (Mitki/Mitki Press). His work has appeared in numerous print and on-line journals and magazines, including *Ploughshares*, *The Threepenny Review*, *Slope*, *Mississippi Review*, and *New York Tyrant*. He has received fellowships from the National Endowment for the Arts and the New York Foundation for the Arts and a grant from the Constance Saltonstall Foundation for the Arts. One of the founding editors of the literary journal *3rd Bed*, he is an associate professor of English at Syracuse University where he directs the MFA Program in Creative Writing.

—m—

BOA Editions, Ltd.
American Poets Continuum Series

No. 1 *The Fuhrer Bunker: A Cycle of Poems in Progress*
W. D. Snodgrass

No. 2 *She*
M. L. Rosenthal

No. 3 *Living With Distance*
Ralph J. Mills, Jr.

No. 4 *Not Just Any Death*
Michael Waters

No. 5 *That Was Then: New and Selected Poems*
Isabella Gardner

No. 6 *Things That Happen Where There Aren't Any People*
William Stafford

No. 7 *The Bridge of Change: Poems 1974–1980*
John Logan

No. 8 *Signatures*
Joseph Stroud

No. 9 *People Live Here: Selected Poems 1949–1983*
Louis Simpson

No. 10 *Yin*
Carolyn Kizer

No. 11 *Duhamel: Ideas of Order in Little Canada*
Bill Tremblay

No. 12 *Seeing It Was So*
Anthony Piccione

No. 13 *Hyam Plutzik: The Collected Poems*

No. 14 *Good Woman: Poems and a Memoir 1969–1980*
Lucille Clifton

No. 15 *Next: New Poems*
Lucille Clifton

No. 16 *Roxa: Voices of the Culver Family*
William B. Patrick

No. 17 *John Logan: The Collected Poems*

No. 18 *Isabella Gardner: The Collected Poems*

No. 19 *The Sunken Lightship*
Peter Makuck

No. 20 *The City in Which I Love You*
Li-Young Lee

No. 21 *Quilting: Poems 1987–1990*
Lucille Clifton

No. 22 *John Logan: The Collected Fiction*

No. 23 *Shenandoah and Other Verse Plays*
Delmore Schwartz

No. 24 *Nobody Lives on Arthur Godfrey Boulevard*
Gerald Costanzo

No. 25 *The Book of Names: New and Selected Poems*
Barton Sutter

No. 26 *Each in His Season*
W. D. Snodgrass

No. 27 *Wordworks: Poems Selected and New*
Richard Kostelanetz

No. 28 *What We Carry*
Dorianne Laux

No. 29 *Red Suitcase*
Naomi Shihab Nye

No. 30 *Song*
Brigit Pegeen Kelly

No. 31 *The Fuehrer Bunker: The Complete Cycle*
W. D. Snodgrass

No. 32 *For the Kingdom*
Anthony Piccione

No. 33 *The Quicken Tree*
Bill Knott

No. 34 *These Upraised Hands*
William B. Patrick

Colophon

Ennui Prophet, poems by Christopher Kennedy, is set
in Adobe Garamond, a digital font designed in 1989
by Robert Slimbach (1956–) based on the French
Renaissance roman types of Claude Garamond (ca. 1480–
1561) and the italics of Robert Granjon (1513–1589).

The publication of this book is made possible, in part,
by the special support of the following individuals:

Anonymous
Joseph Belluck, *in honor of* Bernadette Catalana
Bernadette Catalana
Jonathan Everitt
Pete & Bev French
Anne Germanacos
Janice N. Harrington & Robert Dale Parker
X. J. Kennedy
Jack & Gail Langerak
Rosemary & Lew Lloyd
Boo Poulin
Deborah Ronnen & Sherman Levey
Steven O. Russell & Phyllis Rifkin-Russell
Ellen & David Wallack
Dan & Nan Westervelt, *in honor of* Pat Braus & Ed Lopez
Glenn & Helen William

POETRY
US $16.00

"With the lyricism and clarity of prose poems and the direct narrative drive of short-short stories—and often with a strain of whimsical humor ('I rose from the dead just to see what's for dinner')—the rich and varied pieces in Christopher Kennedy's *Ennui Prophet* carry us into ever new imaginative territory, both fantastical and realistic, each one a fresh departure from the one before. A pleasure to read!"

—Lydia Davis

"The speaker in Christopher Kennedy's prose poems inhabits a world that readers will find at once disturbingly strange and alarmingly familiar. Each day that man is almost destroyed by what he calls 'the daily bloodletting' as he moves through the gauntlet of his surreal humiliations. Almost destroyed, but in the end not, as through these lush imaginings '[t]he maps evolve and the world gets a makeover.'"

—Lucia Perillo

"Comprised entirely of prose poems, Christopher Kennedy's *Ennui Prophet* finds its form in something more organic than writing: the dreaming mind. These oneiric poems are exquisite, at times dark, ludic, roaming: they invite us to hold the crescent moon as a weapon or to hear a quiet sound 'as if a blind carpenter were hammering roses.' This collection is seeded with an immense, almost hallucinatory wonder that makes me want to walk up to complete strangers and say, 'Do you have a minute? There's a poem here I'd like you to read.'"

—Maurice Kilwein Guevara

BOA
EDITIONS LTD
250 N. GOODMAN ST.
SUITE 306
ROCHESTER, NY 14607
WWW.BOAEDITIONS.ORG

ISBN 978-1-934414-49-1

51600

9 781934 414491

9781934414491
ENNUI PROPHET